Seaside Gardening

F. W. SHEPHERD

Cassell
The Royal Horticultural Society

THE ROYAL HORTICULTURAL SOCIETY

Cassell Educational Limited
Villiers House, 41/47 Strand
London WC2N 5JE
for the Royal Horticultural Society

First published 1990

British Library Cataloguing in Publication Data
Shepherd, F. W. (Frederick William),
  Seaside gardening.
  1. Great Britain. Coastal regions. Gardening
  I. Title   II. Series
  635.90941

  ISBN 0-304-31967-8

Photographs by Michael Warren, Harry Smith Collection and Andrew Lawson

The map on p. 9 is Crown Copyright and is reproduced, with minor adaptations, by permission
of the Controller of Her Majesty's Stationery Office

Phototypesetting by Chapterhouse Ltd, Formby
Printed in Hong Kong by Wing King Tong Co. Ltd

Cover: Headland, a clifftop garden in Cornwall
Frontispiece: rock roses like Helianthemum 'Cerise Queen'
flourish in a sunny spot regardless of wind
Back cover: 'Mrs Popple' and other fuchsias are a familiar
sight in seaside areas of the mild southwest (photographs
by Michael Warren)

Contents

Introduction

To those who have visited the seaside – and who has not? – gardening by the sea may bring to mind bright displays of spring bulbs or summer bedding. Others will remember windswept trees and shrubs, with sometimes unfamiliar plants crouching in their lee. But those who have the good fortune to live and garden near the sea will know that the brilliant bedding displays are rarely possible for them, because time and money are not always available and because such displays must be well sheltered from the winds.

The many who think of retiring to a seaside town or village or buying a holiday home on the coast, and who wish to start or continue gardening as a hobby, must appreciate that they will enter a new phase in their gardening experience. In addition to the new problems, mainly caused by the stronger winds, they will still face all the old ones. Weeds, sometimes of a different kind, will continue to grow – frequently, in the milder districts, later in the autumn and earlier in the spring. Diseases and pests still appear. Mowing, quite often right through the winter, and pruning still need attention. Other hobbies, such as sailing and fishing, may also compete.

However, against the problems and distractions of seaside gardening there are advantages that new seaside gardeners should not forget. They can take heart that many plants, probably new to them, thrive in very windy situations, and that other plants, rare in inland Britain except in greenhouses, can be grown in the milder coastal gardens. There are, therefore, two distinct types of garden that can be planned by the seaside gardener. The first, amply sheltered, would include many tender or half-hardy plants, providing new variety of shape, colour and scent; the second would consist entirely of wind-hardy plants needing little attention.

This book sets out to tell of the differences between seaside and inland gardening, to explain the difficulties and to assist in overcoming them. We will limit our scope to those situations that are within reach of onshore winds carrying salt and, in some cases, sand from the shore. We will first consider the two significant climatic factors that affect the seaside garden – immoderate winds and moderate temperatures.

Formal bedding on the seafront at Bridlington, Yorkshire

Wind and Shelter

DAMAGE FROM WIND

The most important feature of the seaside climate is undoubtedly the wind. It is stronger when coming in over the uninterrupted surface of the sea and it picks up salt spume from the waves and, in some places, fine sand from the shore to add to its damaging abilities. Wind may bend, break, scorch, tear and uproot plants and some of this damage is increased when salt and sand are included in the assault. Many good garden plants of inland gardens are not accustomed to such attacks and suffer accordingly, but from the coasts of numerous countries have come plants that survive and even thrive in the presence of wind, salt and blown sand. We will discuss them later, as it is to them that we must turn both for protection and to supply the chief inhabitants of exposed gardens.

In general, wind reduces temperatures. In winter, however, light onshore winds from over the water, which is at a higher temperature than the earth, maintain slightly higher temperatures. Thus, where the sea has an effect, average temperatures are often lower in summer and higher in winter. The provision of shelter reduces wind speeds and the consequent lowering of temperatures, but fortunately does not counteract the warming effect of onshore winter winds (see figure 1, p. 9).

Damage by wind allows fungus diseases to enter and spread more readily in many plants. The spores of some fungi causing plant diseases can only enter the plant through damaged tissue and this is often found on leaves, branches, flowers and fruit that have been exposed to strong winds. At the same time, the moister atmosphere by the sea improves the conditions in which diseases thrive.

Wind-shaped thorns and other trees on the coast suggest long periods of strong gales from off the sea, but the shaping is not usually caused by persistent winds. It is nearly always the result of pruning by the wind, perhaps only once a year, when really strong salt-laden gales kill or shorten all new growth directly exposed to it. After such wind-pruning, the unexposed twigs and branches will

Plumes of the pink pampas grass look particularly fine in the wind and are relatively unharmed by it continue to grow more or less horizontally to leeward and the well known leaning tree will develop.

It must not be thought that winds only flow onshore or from one direction. Even with the so-called prevailing winds, it is rare for more than 40% of the wind to come from one of the four quarters of the compass, or more than 25% from the southwest, which is usually the source of the strongest and most frequent winds. Strong winds can and do come from all quarters. Overland winds may bring less damage than the salt-laden sea winds but, in winter when from the north and east, they may carry snow and frost that are equally damaging.

On the east coast, where the onshore winds are, in winter, the cold winds, protection from their combined effects is even more important. The farther south and west one goes, the less important will be the freezing effects of onshore winds, although salt damage will occur. However, protection will still be needed against winds from other quarters, unless the garden is naturally sheltered by hills or woodlands on the landward side.

THE EFFECT OF BARRIERS

Before looking at the means of providing shelter, let us consider the effect of barriers on windspeed and direction. Wind is, of course, air moving from an area of high pressure to one of lower pressure. It moves more or less directly and at more or less even speeds over water or flat land, but swerves and eddies when obstacles of any kind are interposed. Wind cannot be stopped, but it can be deflected or filtered.

A solid barrier deflects wind and, when this happens, the speed increases over the top and at the ends of the barrier. This can often be noticed at street corners or between two solid hedges, where the wind is diverted and the air whistles round or through at greater speeds. Immediately behind a solid barrier, there will be an area of comparative calm; further away, the wind will drive downwards from the high pressure area in front of and above the obstacle to a relatively low pressure space from which the air has been kept by the barrier. Thus, in the lee of a solid windbreak some shelter can be found, but a little beyond it there will be an area of turbulence and wind eddying where more damage will be caused to plants and other vulnerable objects.

A permeable barrier, on the other hand, allows some wind to pass through at reduced speeds, while sending some of it over the top or around the ends in the same way as a solid wall. It will be obvious

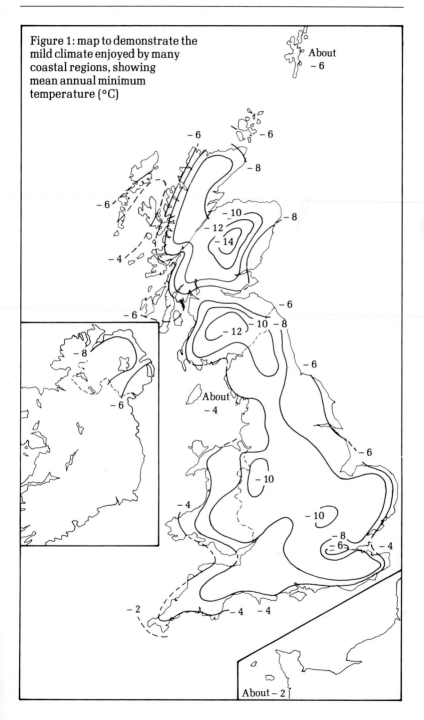

Figure 1: map to demonstrate the mild climate enjoyed by many coastal regions, showing mean annual minimum temperature (°C)

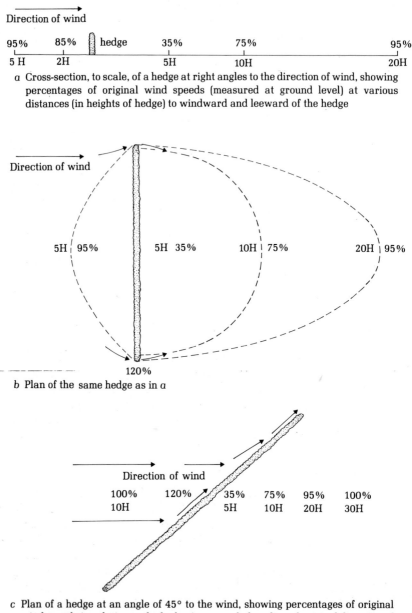

a Cross-section, to scale, of a hedge at right angles to the direction of wind, showing percentages of original wind speeds (measured at ground level) at various distances (in heights of hedge) to windward and leeward of the hedge

b Plan of the same hedge as in *a*

c Plan of a hedge at an angle of 45° to the wind, showing percentages of original wind speeds in relation to the hedge (measured along line of original direction of the wind and not at right angles to the hedge)

Figure 2: the effect of a permeable barrier on wind speeds

that wire netting or similar very permeable screening will allow much of the wind to pass through at almost the original wind speed, whereas a thickish hedge will allow far less to pass through and at considerably reduced speeds, although it may cause some eddying to leeward.

Much research has been conducted into the behaviour of wind and it is known that the optimum permeability for a shelter is about 60% solid to 40% aperture. This significantly reduces wind speeds but causes little turbulence. The lath fences once widely used to protect flower crops in the West Country, and still available in a few places, are near this optimum degree of permeability. The wooden laths, 1 in. (2.5 cm) wide and spaced 1 in. apart, plus the cross-timbers on which they are mounted and the broad bracing diagonals, produce a ratio of about 60:40.

The diagrams in figure 2 illustrate patterns of the wind when blowing against a permeable barrier such as a hedge, trellis or screen. It must be remembered that they are somewhat simplified. Each situation will be different and may produce areas of exposure or shelter that need to be studied on the ground and taken into account before planning any additional protection.

As well as its permeability, the height of a barrier (expressed as H) has a direct relation to wind speed. Quite simply, a solid barrier will give good shelter up to a distance of 2H (i.e. twice the height of the barrier) and there will then be an area of turbulence up to 7H away. A barrier of 60:40 permeability (as shown in the diagrams) will produce little turbulence and will reduce wind speed at ground level up to a distance of about 20H, but with the maximum protection only within about 5H.

PROVIDING SHELTER

Armed with this knowledge of the effect of shelter on wind, and bearing in mind the necessity of good shelter for almost all seaside gardens, how do we set about providing it? As always, each situation will need special attention, depending on its size, slope, shape, aspect and the surrounding shelter and on the wishes of the gardener. Larger gardens, of more than say 50 yd (45 m) across, will probably require tall shelter belts of suitable trees, while in smaller gardens, living hedges or artificial fences will be necessary.

Most gardeners will wish to preserve any existing attractive views from the house or garden. The competition between the pleasure of the scenery and protection from the wind has to be faced in almost all seaside gardens, with the additional problem of reduced sunshine and increased shade caused by shelter, particularly on the east and west where the shadows are long. Short of having a well sheltered garden with little or no view or, alternatively, ample views but little wind protection, the only solution is to provide several low screens at intervals across the garden over which the eye can roam to any distant horizons.

Shelter belts

A shelter belt may be defined as two or more rows of trees unpruned and growing to their full height and spread. Three rows are often recommended and even wider belts have been planted in exposed country, usually for the protection of farmsteads or livestock and the ultimate production of timber. Two rows will suffice for most garden purposes and, taking a long term view, will enable a third row to be planted some years later when the first two are beginning to become thin at the bottom.

× *Cupressocyparis leylandii* 'Castlewellan' makes a good tall hedge or shelter belt, but is less vigorous than the Leyland cypress itself

Young, suitably spaced trees will soon provide some shelter and, when mature, they will give permeable shelter and good protection for the garden and the plants established in their lee. The area protected obviously increases as the trees grow. Thus, when they are 50 ft (15 m) high, land up 250 ft (76 m) away in the lee of the belt can be well protected and there will be some protection at up to 1000 ft (305 m) away. Trees take time to grow and we cannot all afford the time allowed by Osgood Mackenzie, at Inverewe in the north of Scotland, who planted *Pinus radiata* and then left it for some 25 years before planting his garden! Useful shelter will usually be produced within ten years and meanwhile temporary artificial shelter or quick-growing hedges can be used and, if necessary, removed as the shelter belt becomes effective.

Trees for a shelter belt or for any other purpose in windy situations are best planted as young seedlings or even younger plants from cuttings. Older, large trees have too much top in relation to the amount of root, making them likely to be blown over by strong winds, and staking is expensive and often useless in exposed positions. The seedlings may be described as 1 + 1 plants in catalogues, which means that they have spent one year in the seed bed and one year lined out before being lifted for planting in their permanent positions. Very few trees are raised from cuttings, the most noteworthy exception being the hybrid Leyland cypress (see p. 14). Young plants should have the opportunity of making good new root systems before the tops become too large and top-heavy. They will benefit from protection in the early years when establishing themselves (see p.17) and also need to be kept clean and free from weeds.

Thorough cultivation of the ground and the elimination of perennial weeds in a strip of land 12 ft (3.6 m) wide are good preparation for a two-row shelter belt. The young trees, in their two, or at most, three rows, should be planted as 'staggered' rows and not opposite each other. For most species, 6 ft (1.8 m) each way is a suitable distance. Towards the end of winter is probably the best time for planting and firming in. Earlier planting may lead to loosening during a long wet winter and later planting may be followed by a dry spell that makes establishment difficult. After planting, application of a residual herbicide such as simazine, between the trees but not on them, will help them to make a good start without competition from weeds. There should be no further cultivation of the ground because this could damage the roots and loosen the soil around them, which might result in the young trees being blown over before they were properly established.

After the first year of clean ground and following the application of simazine or a similar weedkiller, grass may be sown between the rows. This will curb weeds and hold the roots of the trees firmly in place, but it should not be sown right up to their stems. In a few years, no further restriction of weeds will be necessary. The grass may need cutting for another year or two, or until the overgrowth of tree branches keeps it in check, and weeds around the base may require attention if they are growing so tall as to shade and damage the lowest branches of the young trees. Thereafter, ordinary garden weeds will do little harm to the trees. The worst weeds in a shelter belt are such competing plants as brambles, ivy, elder, thorn, ash and sycamore, which should be dealt with as soon as they appear.

The choice of trees to form a shelter belt by the sea is limited. As with so many decisions in gardening, a careful study of neigh-bouring plantings and a word or two with those who garden in the locality will be helpful. The most effective trees are evergreens, which will give protection all the year round. In the south and west of Britain, the quick-growing, massive Monterey pine, *Pinus radiata*, from a very limited district on the west coast of North America, is as good as any. Singed by salt spray but quickly recovering and remaining upright and firm at the roots, it grows 2 ft (60 cm) or more each year after becoming established. The beach pine, *P. contorta*, comes from a much wider area of the west of the United States and Canada, with consequent variations in growth and usefulness. The variety *latifolia*, known as the lodgepole pine, is the one usually planted for shelter purposes in this country. It probably survives colder conditions and is therefore more widely used in the colder parts of the country.

When closely clipped, as it so often is, the Monterey cypress, *Cupressus macrocarpa*, is a great disappointment, but when allowed to grow untrimmed as a shelter-belt tree, it is one of the toughest of all trees for the seaside in the mildest regions. The Leyland cypress, × *Cupressocyparis leylandii*, has been widely planted in recent years and somewhat maligned for its instability. Like all the others, only very young trees must be planted. Being a hybrid and raised from cuttings, there is no tap root and the two or three main roots tend to grow horizontally. Newly rooted cuttings (never transplants or plants raised overlong in containers) should be permanently planted as soon as the site is clean and deeply

Pinus contorta var. *latifolia*, a reliable shelter-belt tree for coastal sites

cultivated. Only then will the roots spread quickly and a little down-wards to support the rapidly growing tops. Shallow soils over chalk or rock are not suitable for this tree, as the roots do not seem able to penetrate into the lower crevices as do those of some of the pines.

The European evergreen oak, or holm oak, *Quercus ilex*, is slower-growing than any of the others already mentioned, but is just as stable when properly planted and longer-lived. It is distinctive in form and growth. Probably the main cause for complaint in tidy gardens is that it sheds its considerable load of leaves in the spring and early summer when all thoughts of leaf-collecting have long since passed.

Among deciduous trees, ash, *Fraxinus excelsior*, and sycamore, *Acer pseudoplatanus*, will provide some protection on exposed sites, although they will always be wind-shaped near the coast and therefore less effective than the evergreens. The loss of leaves in the winter reduces their efficiency as shelter, but this may be useful if the plants or garden only require shelter in the summer. There may be some advantage also in that the leafless trees allow a little more light into the sheltered area.

Shelter-belt trees are just as much living, growing and, later, decaying features as any other plants. They need regular if not frequent attention – the removal of weeds in the shape of competing trees and of broken branches and dead trees if they occur. All shelter belts are best thinned as they grow. This will enable the remaining plants to grow into massive trees that will stand firm and provide shelter for a long time to come. The gardener arriving in an established garden is more likely to face these problems of maintenance than one who has recently planted a shelter belt.

At some stage, almost every shelter belt will become thin at the bottom, leading to wind damage through the gaps. This can often be overcome, if there is space, by planting an additional row of trees of the same or similar species. They are planted just beyond the spreading branches of the original trees, within the span of the roots, and individual preparation of the place for each tree will be necessary. Where there is a choice, the lighter side of the shelter belt is preferable, enabling the young trees to make reasonable growth and gradually merge into the existing line.

The alternative is to plant one of the rather few shrubs that will grow well under all but the heaviest shade. Thick pines are unlikely to permit such plantings to succeed, but an existing open shelter belt may well benefit from infilling. There is one attractive evergreen shrub, *Griselinia littoralis*, that will grow beneath moderate shade in the mildest parts and fill in gaps between trees (see p. 22).

Sea buckthorn, *Hippophae rhamnoides*, is useful by the sea as an outer screen or wind-hardy shrub

Although not frost-hardy, it will also make a very useful hedge in the open in warmer coastal districts. Other shrubs that can be used for infilling are native holly, *Ilex aquifolium*, and some of the evergreen oleasters, including *Elaeagnus × ebbingei*, *E. pungens* and several of its variegated forms, and *E. × reflexa*. The latter, in particular, tends to produce climbing branches that may eventually smother the main trees if these are not growing very vigorously. If the site of the shelter belt is very exposed, any underplanting of shrubs or additional rows of trees will almost certainly need some artificial shelter in their first few years.

Outer screens
The importance of protecting young trees in a shelter belt while they become established has already been mentioned. In the teeth of the wind, near the shore or cliff edge, any rough vegetation will be welcome protection for a newly planted shelter belt or more formal hedges. Native gorse, elder, sycamore, sea buckthorn, ash, blackthorn and quickthorn, with the inevitable brambles, may be left 3–6 ft (0.9–1.8 m) wide where there is space on the windward side of the plants. They will be singed and tattered and, although

17

never reaching any great height, will provide some protection in the first years. They will later prove the point that there is some shelter on the windward side of windbreaks, and will be seen to grow taller than normal as the shelter belt too makes growth.

If it can be established, the New Zealand flax, *Phormium tenax*, will stand boldly in exposed situations (see p. 33). So also will some bamboos, particularly *Pseudosasa (Arundinaria) japonica*. They will look bedraggled after every storm, but will send up new growth each spring that will provide some shelter at the lower levels. Bamboos are particularly good in moist rich soil (see p. 56).

Hedges

A single row of trees or shrubs, trimmed to a predetermined height and breadth, can make a formal hedge. A single row of shrubs, or of a mixture of shrubs, left untrimmed, becomes an informal hedge. Almost any shrub can be used for an informal hedge, although the number that will survive in seaside conditions is much smaller. Shrubs that can be clipped to formal hedges are less plentiful and, of these, very few indeed can be planted by the sea.

As with a shelter belt, good soil preparation and the removal of perennial weeds, and using young plants and keeping them weed-free all contribute to the early and successful establishment of a hedge. When possible, planting a hedge against small-mesh wire netting or similar screening encourages more rapid and upright growth. Weeds must be controlled as they compete for food and water, so reducing the rate of growth and, what is worse, may smother the lower branches and leave them permanently bare. A single row of hedge plants is easier to keep weed-free and is less costly than a double row, which has no real advantage.

Most of the suitable hedge shrubs may be planted 1–3 ft (30–90 cm) apart and, except for those intended to form a single stem, such as certain conifers, they are best hard-pruned after the first year of growth. This involves the removal of at least half the length of the leading shoots and trimming the more or less horizontal shoots to leave them 6–8 in. (15–20 cm) long. The initial pruning will encourage a good thick bottom to the young hedge and, as the seasons pass, trimming should be designed to produce a broad base and narrow top. This shape not only tends to preserve the lower branches, because they receive more light than when the sides are vertical or undercut (as so many hedges are), but also reduces the risk of the tops being broken out by heavy snow. With the bottom forming a solid barrier and the top a permeable one, a hedge of this kind makes an almost ideal shelter, with good protection at ground level and a filtering top that reduces wind turbulence.

The range of seaside shrubs that can be considered for use as hedges is greater than that of trees for shelter belts, but they are still few in comparison with the number available for planting inland. The genus *Escallonia*, from the shores of South America, contains some of the best seaside hedges, especially *E. rubra* var. *macrantha* and the two cultivars raised in Cornwall, 'Crimson Spire' and 'Red Hedger'. These are wind- and salt-tolerant and fairly frost-hardy. Many of the others are too flimsy or more tender and, although they make attractive semi-formal hedges, are not really suitable for providing shelter. The cheapest method of forming an escallonia hedge is to plant cuttings in a single row from late October onwards, having prepared the strip of ground for the hedge early in the autumn. The cuttings, of current year's growth up to 12 in. (30 cm) long, are inserted with at least two thirds of their length in the soil and about 1 ft (30 cm) apart. They should not be pushed in as this is likely to damage the base and impede rooting. In

Some escallonias provide excellent seaside hedges

most circumstances, the cuttings will have rooted by the spring and some growth will have appeared by the autumn. They may then be lightly pruned and, if kept free from weeds, are quite able to reach 6 ft (1.8 m) in height within three years of planting. Plants raised elsewhere from cuttings and planted in their permanent site in the spring may suffer some setback, but soon become established to attain a similar height if conditions are good.

Escallonias may be clipped twice or more each year, when they have made good growth in the early summer and again in the early autumn, and will then form a solid evergreen hedge rivalling close-clipped yew or privet in appearance. Clipped only once a year, in July, they produce short growth before the winter and carry a striking display of red flowers in late spring and early summer. They may be 'burnt' by strong gales and lose many of their leaves in the coldest winters, but will recover the following spring.

In addition to the oleasters for use in partially shaded conditions (p. 17), some others including the deciduous *Elaeagnus angustifolia* and *E. umbellata* may be trimmed into quite useful hedges, resisting much of the wind that may be experienced by the sea. Trimming once a year during the late summer will keep them moderately formal, while left untouched they form a strong but spreading barrier. They are not quite so quick-growing in the early stages as escallonias, but when established many make rapid growth.

Some of the numerous New Zealand olearias are useful hedges in

Tamarix ramosissima 'Rosea' thrives in exposed coastal places

the milder districts, although they are generally better when untrimmed as informal barriers. They are evergreen, with small daisy-like flowers, and mostly very wind-hardy. *Olearia* × *haastii* is the hardiest and thrives inland in the north of England, but it is not very tall or quick-growing. It can be made into a neat formal hedge, of up to about 5 ft (1.5 m) high, almost anywhere. With grey holly-like leaves and broad panicles of small white flowers in June and July, *O. macrodonta* is more satisfactory as an informal hedge up to 15 ft (4.5 m) high than when close-trimmed (see p. 29). If killed to the ground in very cold winters, it usually grows again from the base. *Olearia virgata* behaves in the same way, growing even more rapidly after being cut back by a very sharp frost. It has the advantage that, although not looking very ornamental, the dead branches will remain in place to provide some shelter while the new growth is appearing. This shrub has somewhat rosemary-like leaves and an upright habit and is best left untrimmed to withstand the severest gales. Even faster-growing but even less frost-hardy is *O. traversii*, which is quite often killed except in the mildest districts. It is so quick-growing that its roots rarely keep it erect unless it is strongly staked or hard-pruned in the early years to reduce the imbalance between root and top growth. Nevertheless, planted young against good artificial shelter and with half its annual growth removed in the first three years, it makes a most attractive and useful hedge in warmer areas.

Several others daisy bushes, such as *Olearia albida*, *O. avicennii-folia*, *O. paniculata*, with wavy-edged leaves rather like *Pittosporum tenuifolium*, and *O. solandri*, looking like a tall golden-leaved heather, may be used as mostly quite narrow, informal hedges in suitable climates. From the related genus *Senecio*, *S. reinoldii* has some of the toughest wind-resistant leaves of any New Zealand shrub, but is better when allowed to form a rounded shrub than when trimmed in an effort to make a formal hedge. It has been known to succumb in sharp frosts. Other lower-growing and somewhat spreading senecios are also wind-hardy and some are more frost-hardy. *Senecio greyi*, *S. monroi*, and the hybrid *S. 'Sunshine'*, evergreens with grey foliage and yellow flowers, would make informal lines of low-growing protection where taller hedges are not wanted.

Euonymus japonicus is usually undamaged by the worst gales and is frost-hardy in most parts of the country. Strange as it may seem, the exception is in the milder areas, where the plant goes on growing long into the autumn and, when this growth is hit by a sharp frost in the new year, is killed back to the older wood. It is, however, a most useful evergreen hedge plant – if not a very attractive one – for almost all seaside gardens. There are also variegated cultivars.

The tamarisks are well known seaside shrubs, deciduous, wind-hardy, frost-resistant and providing good permeable shelter. They have been trimmed to make semi-formal hedges, but do not survive long in that condition. There are several species – *Tamarix gallica*, being regarded as a denizen of this country, and *T. parviflora*, *T. ramosissima* (*T. pentandra*; see p. 20) and *T. tetrandra* from southern Europe and western Africa – all of which will serve well as informal screens or even thrive in the outer defences with the commoner natives (see p. 17).

Of other shrubs that can be used as more or less formal hedges in the milder districts, *Griselinia littoralis* (p. 16) has a very compact root system, which makes it easy to transplant as quite a large

Griselinia littoralis, a versatile seaside shrub that can be used as a hedge, filler or in its own right

shrub. *Fuchsia magellanica* var. *gracilis* and *F.* 'Riccartonii' are attractive flowering hedges in seaside areas of the southwest. The latter is the stronger and will reach 6 ft (1.8 m) in two or three years when the winters are relatively frost-free. They usually grow again from below ground after hard frosts have struck and, in the warmer parts, will reach even double that height. *Pittosporum tenuifolium* stands a certain amount of wind in milder regions, but needs complete protection when it is being grown for its evergreen foliage. Stronger-growing and altogether more wind-resistant are *P. crassifolium* and *P. ralphii*, but they are quite tender and really only suitable as hedges, for which they are used in the Isles of Scilly. *Muehlenbeckia complexa*, sometimes known as the wire netting plant, has very thin wiry stems that will scramble upwards and over any plant or fence and quickly makes an almost impenetrable mass of twining shoots in milder areas. Some of the dwarfer and close-growing hebes, such as the *Hebe* × *franciscana* hybrids, are sufficiently wind-hardy to make useful low hedges near the coast.

Artificial shelter

Walls and stone-faced banks make permanent boundaries and provide solid shelter that can be useful in protecting trees and shrubs while they are becoming established. Wooden fences of various kinds, including the standard lath fences (p. 11), wire and plastic netting and various other plastic fences all make good temporary screens against which hedge shrubs can grow more readily to serviceable heights (see p. 24).

Where a fence forms the boundary between two plots, it is always as well to talk to the neighbour before making any planting on or adjacent to the boundary. If complete agreement is reached, the new hedge may be planted as close to the boundary as possible and will grow through the fence to be trimmed by each on their own side. After all, most people want a good hedge and a single line of one kind is far better than two, which often make the hedge so wide that trimming of the top becomes almost impossible. The temporary and sometimes not very sightly fences can then be absorbed in the hedge, improving the appearance of the garden and retaining its original purpose of defining the boundary and keeping out unwanted cats and dogs. However, if the neighbour insists on a different hedge or wishes to see only the fence, it may be necessary to plant the hedge or shelter belt some distance from the boundary, to allow enough room to prune the plants on your own side and to prevent the trees or shrubs from growing over the neighbour's land.

Whatever is chosen as a temporary artificial fence, it is of the

greatest importance that the stakes and other supports are adequate. A fence that stands and provides shelter for almost the whole year and then blows over in an exceptional gale is worse than useless. This is because many plants, when protected from wind, expand and grow more openly than they would without shelter and if, after a year of good growth, the protection is suddenly removed, the damage is greater than ever. So stout supporting posts should be deeply set in the ground, with struts or wires all strongly held together by screws or nails, and should enable the fence to withstand the occasional hurricane. Remember, too, that gales often bring rain and that the additional weight of the water makes fences even heavier and more difficult to support.

ACHIEVING AND MAINTAINING ADEQUATE SHELTER

It is not always possible to ensure that shelter is of the optimum 60% permeability, particularly with shelter belts and hedges, which vary with the seasons and conditions and as the plants grow. Measuring their permeability is also very difficult.

Viewed from right angles, a shelter belt or hedge may appear quite solid and, from a more acute angle, very solid, but when the leaves and branches move in the wind, it may actually be too open or permeable. However, observation of the effect of the wind on plants in the lee side will provide a clue as to whether the shelter is sufficient. As a general rule, it may be said that, if moving figures can be seen but not identified through a hedge or shelter belt, the amount of shelter is about right and no changes need be attempted.

If a hedge is too solid, it may be thinned by trimming more closely to remove the mesh of small twigs that thicken it; if it is too open, one or both sides may be trimmed less closely for a year or more. It is less easy to improve a shelter belt, which is not trimmed, although the main fault – gaps at the bottom – can usually be overcome by additional planting (see p. 16).

Rigid artificial shelter in the form of lath or similar wood fences can be measured to assess the degree of permeability. Unlike a living screen, it will not alter. Flexible shelter, such as plastic fencing, may be less effective than it appears because it gives way under pressure, allowing more wind to blow through and at greater speeds to cause increased damage on the lee side. Additional layers of material should then be provided for reinforcement.

Above: plastic netting creates a serviceable windbreak
Below: a fine bedding display at Torquay, Devon

Types of Seaside Garden

Having considered the main problem of seaside gardening – the wind and how to reduce its effect – let us consider the gardening alternatives that can be practised by the sea. The various forms of gardening to be found in Britain are so numerous as to be almost endless, depending as they do on the wishes of the owner and on the size and conditions of the plot. Where there is room, a framework of trees and many shrubs among lawns can provide a reasonably work-free garden. Add herbaceous flower and bulbs and the work required will increase, while even more labour is necessary with biennials and annuals, whether sown or bedded. Almost all these types of ornamental gardening will need good protection in windy conditions. Alpine or rock gardening perhaps needs less shelter, as many alpines come from fairly exposed situations, but the plants demand quite a lot of attention to keep them in order and weed-free.

Enthusiasts for individual plants or groups of plants are widespread. One has seen gardens of roses, of irises and even of pelargoniums, and many gardeners devote their energies to chrysanthemums, dahlias, sweet peas or daffodils. If, as is often the case, the purpose of the specialism is exhibition, the need for shelter is paramount. The same applies to growing hardy fruit, for one's own use, and vegetables, if the show bench is in mind, when wind damage can be very limiting.

We will return briefly to the special needs of these various gardens in seaside conditions, but there are really two possibilities by the sea that should be considered – a garden of wind-hardy plants; or a garden consisting of plants only on the verge of hardiness, which have, in the past, tempted so many gardeners in the mildest districts.

THE WINDSWEPT GARDEN

Before shelter is established or even without any intention of providing it, the gardener may rely entirely on wind-hardy plants for the framework or the whole of the garden. Such an unsheltered garden can be economical of time and energy, requiring little

The Brazilian *Tibouchina urvilleana*, a tempting shrub for gardeners in warm districts by the sea pruning, clipping, staking or tying and generally smothering most weeds, thus reducing the amount of weeding and hoeing. It does however, lack many of the well loved features of other gardens. It is quite unsuitable for most of the usual herbaceous plants, annuals or bedding plants, and fruit and vegetable gardening is more or less impossible. It can be open and sunny on the few calm bright days, but is not tempting to work in or for relaxation on the many days when wind is blowing.

Lawns

If the garden is large enough, there may be space, on a suitably maintained lawn, for garden sports. Bowls and croquet do not need the formality of a rectangular plot and can be played on an irregular lawn among beds and borders of shrubs. A single rink for bowls should be 42 × 7 yd (38 × 6 m), although a full green must be 42 × 42 yd (38 × 38 m) with adequate surrounds. Croquet requires 32 × 28 yd (29 × 25 m), but enjoyable games can be had on other sizes and shapes. About 40 × 22 yd (36 × 20 m) overall is necessary for lawn tennis, with enough surrounding netting if the game is not to become too exhausting from chasing errant balls to all parts of the garden. Golf putting can be accommodated on quite a small lawn and does not need the careful levelling of some other games, but the grass must be finely cut and any competitive matches take up an extensive area.

Shrubs

There is a range of wind-hardy and attractive plants which can fill the windswept garden and which, as time passes, will provide sheltered pockets where even greater variety can be introduced. Where there is room, any of the trees and shrubs already mentioned as suitable for giving shelter and many of their relatives may be planted in borders, groups or as individual specimens around and in ample lawns, to form a pleasant, easily run garden. Less space obviously makes it impossible to use trees or larger shrubs, but there are others to enhance even a small garden.

Of the considerable number of species and cultivars of escallonia, most are evergreens and make rounded shrubs, some with arching branches. The colour range is from the intense white against shining foliage of 'Iveyi' – one of the tallest – through many pinks, including the well named 'Apple Blossom' and 'Peach Blossom', to the deep reds of the glossy-leaved *Escallonia rubra* var. *macrantha* and its hybrids, including E. 'C. F. Ball'. Most escallonias are generous with their small flowers and are covered with colour for several weeks, from late May, when E. 'Pride of Donard' commences, to October when E. 'C. F. Ball' and others finish.

The oleasters also make strong, solid, rounded shrubs with handsome foliage but inconspicuous flowers. *Elaeagnus × ebbingei* has striking shining leaves which are silvery beneath and the somewhat similar *E. pungens* has a number of variegated cultivars that add all-the-year interest to the garden. There are several others that are sufficiently different to provide variety in a windswept garden (see also pp.17 and 20). All produce small white flowers in the late summer and well into the autumn, giving a pleasant perfume at that time of the year.

Few of the olearias (p. 21) are sufficiently frost-hardy to be included in the unsheltered windswept garden, except in the mildest climates, but where they can be relied upon, they will contribute their attractive, daisy-like, slightly scented flowers to the scene.

Two of the large-leaved senecios, *Senecio reinoldii* and *S. elaeagnifolius*, are well able to withstand the strongest of winds, but have been killed to the ground in colder winters. Another large shrub,

Olearia macrodonta withstands wind, but may be cut back by severe cold

Cotton lavender flowers throughout the summer, given a position in full sun

almost a tree as it ages, *Griselinia littoralis* (p. 16) has pale bold foliage and is a good plant for the exposed garden.

The more compact lavenders and the cotton lavender, *Santolina chamaecyparissus*, remain unharmed in windy situations. Other grey foliage shrubs that grow well in salt-laden winds include the rock roses, *Helianthemum* and *Halimium*, with similar single rose-like flowers. Several of the small-leaved cotoneasters are low wind-resisters, with white flowers in spring and coloured leaves and berries in autumn. *Cotoneaster horizontalis* really needs a wall or bank against which to spread itself, but *C. microphyllus*, *C. dammeri*, *C. adpressus* and *C. conspicuus* are all admirable for the front of the border. Many of the heathers – *Erica* and *Calluna* species and cultivars – are sufficiently wind-resistant, provided the soil is not

The striking *Yucca gloriosa* 'Variegata' is frost-hardy

alkaline. As can be seen in a number of well known gardens, including the RHS Garden, Wisley, heathers can be a most attractive feature in the right surroundings. Their wide range of flowering periods and extensive spectrum of foliage colours enable a garden of great variety to be planned (see also the Wisley handbook, *Heaths and heathers*).

The native sea buckthorn, *Hippophae rhamnoides*, grows best on sandy shores, but is useful anywhere by the sea and provides a more open form than many of the shrubs already described, with decorative orange fruits during the winter. Several of the yuccas, with their sharp leaves and striking spikes of white flowers, are valuable for contrasting with the solid shapes of wind-hardy shrubs. In the same way, bamboos will break the line of shrubby borders (see p. 56). They will look rather tatty after the fiercest gales, but produce a new crop of shoots each year. The rounded outline of a single plant of the pampas grass, *Cortaderia selloana*, is relieved in early autumn by its spectacular plumes, the clear white of 'Sunningdale Silver' being among the most striking. These may be battered rather earlier in the winter than in more sheltered gardens, but will have served a useful purpose for a while (see p. 6).

Bulbs

Within the framework of hardy shrubs, much colour and interest can be added from the start by planting bulbs which, together, can provide flowers for some nine months of the year. Crocuses can be chosen to flower from autumn to spring in varying colours, starting with the many forms of *Crocus speciosus* and its relations in October and ending with the popular yellow *C. flavus* and its garden hybrids in March. The so-called autumn crocus, *Colchicum autumnale*, and its many relations produce the first crocus-type flowers from September onwards, but they have large, rather intrusive leaves the following spring. Two other crocus-like bulbs are the bright yellow *Sternbergia lutea*, flowering in the autumn, and the reddish purple *Bulbocodium vernum* in early spring. The numerous forms of snowdrop, *Galanthus*, can be had from January through to March and there is also an autumn snowdrop, *G. reginae-olgae*.

In the mildest gardens, daffodils can be in flower from late autumn through to May. *Narcissus* 'Scilly White', found against many south-facing walls, and the Dutch yellow trumpet daffodil, *N.* 'Rijnveld's Early Sensation', flower in early January. Others continue through to the time when *N.* 'Double White' finishes the season as the earliest tulips appear. In all but large gardens, the smaller daffodils are best. The species *N. minimus*, *N. cyclamineus*, *N. bulbocodium*, *N. jonquilla*, *N. triandrus* and the native *N. pseudo-narcissus*, with all their numerous cultivars, may be damaged by the strongest winds, but will provide some colour every year in the shelter of developing shrubs. Most of them are best in short grass which is not cut until the leaves are dying in July (see also the Wisley handbook, *Daffodils*).

Many tulips are not so happy in their ability either to stand the wind or to persist unlifted for many years. However, some of the dwarf, so called botanical tulips are worth including for flowering

New Zealand flax, *Phormium*, makes good wind-resistant clumps

in the late spring before the larger ones. *Tulipa batalinii,*
T. clusiana, T. fosteriana, T. greigii, T. kaufmanniana and others,
with their smaller hybrids, bring a range of colour when grown in
sun with some shelter. The specialist bulb catalogues will suggest
many more less common bulbs that can give interest and colour
throughout the summer until the montbretias (now grouped under
Tritonia and *Crocosmia*) come into flower in late summer and
autumn. The mildest gardens will also allow the planting and
flowering of two different plants sometimes known as naked ladies
– *Amaryllis belladonna* and the nerines. Both flower in warm places
from late August through to late October (see also the Wisley
handbook, *Growing dwarf bulbs.*)

Thus, for the gardener who will accept the limitations of the effect
of the wind, there are many hardy trees and shrubs that can create
the framework of a not too labour-intensive garden, which will
consolidate into an attractive maturity making even less demands
on time and energy. If greater variety and colour are required in the
early years, numerous bulbs can provide them.

THE HALF-HARDY GARDEN

Turning now from the really windswept to the more sheltered
garden, let us consider the possibilities, particularly in the milder
southern and western districts. As we have noted, the shelter may
be provided by natural features of hills and woods, or it may have
been introduced in the forms already described. Apart from the
wind, the other main factor that may limit plant growth will be soil.
As in any garden, chalk, limestone, or, near the sea, most blown
sand with its particles of broken seashells, will usually restrict
ornamental gardening to plants that will grow in alkaline conditions. This eliminates camellias, rhododendrons and most other
ericaceous plants and applies to much but not all of the coast. Badly
drained soils are inhibiting too, but this condition can generally be
overcome. Soils of whatever type may also be shallow over solid
rock or too much broken stone. This is difficult for gardening of any
kind and adds to the problems of establishing and maintaining good
shelter belts where they are needed. However, thorough
preparation of the sites for planting and no further disturbance of
the surface will do much to overcome the handicap.
　　Where there is shelter and the climate is less harsh than normal,
there is a great temptation to try to grow the many attractive plants
that thrive in warmer countries or are to be found under glass

The lovely *Magnolia liliiflora* grows to about 10 ft (3 m) high and across

elsewhere. Such plants often survive and even flourish for several years and then succumb in the severe winters that occur periodically – as in 1946/47, 1962/63, 1981/82 and, in south and west Cornwall and Scilly, in the early weeks of 1987. Gardens can be devastated when short sharp conditions assail tender plants, but not all is lost because some are merely killed above ground level and others are damaged only on the last year's growth that has gone on developing long into the mild autumns. It is a risk that many gardeners in the warmer regions are prepared to take.

Trees, shrubs and wall shrubs
Among the trees and shrubs that prefer sheltered mild conditions are some that are reasonably hardy but benefit from the milder springs in which to flower without the risk of damage from late frosts. They also enjoy the higher rainfall that usually occurs in these parts of the country. Magnolias, particularly those that grow into tall trees, such as *Magnolia campbellii* and var. *mollicomata*, *M. delavayi*, and M. × *veitchii*, are really at their best in open woodland by the sea. Similarly, the medium-sized species such as *M. liliiflora*, *M. sinensis*, M. × *watsonii* and *M. wilsonii* are more likely to flower successfully in the milder areas.

The earliest rhododendrons require protection from wind and also have a greater chance of displaying their flowers to perfection in mild gardens where late frosts are less common. This large genus provides great variety of size, colour and time of flowering, shape and size of leaf, but almost all need an acid soil. They range from the towering *Rhododendron arboreum* and some relatives, reaching 40 ft (12 m) in height, to *R. radicans* and *R. forrestii*, clinging no more than a few inches above the ground. There are red flowers of every hue, through pinks to pure white, with orange and similar colours and some nearly blue among the purples and mauves. They first appear before Christmas and some go on well into the summer. The leaves vary from those almost 20 by 8 in. (50 by 20 cm) of *R. grande* and others in the same group to the tiny leaves of some azaleas, with a variety of greens on the surface and bronzes and darker colours beneath. Several species from southeast Asia are too tender for any outside garden in Britain, but a few that are borderline will survive for many years. *Rhododendron nuttallii*, *R. veitchianum*, *R. virgatum*, *R.* 'Countess of Haddington' and *R.* 'Fragrantissimum' are among those that provide scent and colour where shelter from wind and frost can be given (see also the Wisley handbook, *Rhododendrons*).

Camellias, once grown as greenhouse or conservatory shrubs, have long been found quite hardy in most parts of the country, but they need protection from strong winds and are usually at their best where mild springs will not damage their flowers. Their shining foliage is attractive all the time and the white, pink or red flowers of the numerous cultivars may, in the milder districts, last from November to May (see also the Wisley handbook, *Camellias*).

Many of the wattles or acacias will grow and flower well for a few years, only to be killed in the occasional cold spell. Even then, they may only be cut back to the ground, leaving a number of new growths to appear near, and sometimes at a distance from, the base. Some are useful wall shrubs, although the mimosa, *Acacia dealbata*, which is probably the hardiest, makes quite a thick trunk and is really too strong to grow beside the average wall. *Acacia armata*, *A. longifolia*, *A. rhetinodes* and *A. verticillata* are other wattles that may be planted in the mildest gardens, either against a wall or in a sheltered corner.

There are several most attractive abutilons which thrive in warm districts. *Abutilon vitifolium*, with large, open, lavender-coloured

The fast-growing mimosa, *Acacia dealbata*, flowers in early spring

flowers and deeper purple and white forms, is so fast-growing and floriferous that it should be tried wherever some mild winters can be expected. It grows to at least 10 ft (3 m) in a very few years, to make a striking display in early summer, but, even without frost-damage, its natural life seems to be short, since a plant will die suddenly after a very free-flowering season. Replacements can be raised easily from cuttings – of the cultivars and hybrids – or by seed, and these quickly fill any gaps. *Abutilon megapotamicum* is another rather straggling, tender shrub, with somewhat fuchsia-like flowers of yellow and red. It does best against a south-facing wall and then survives most winters. It can be in flower for some eighteen months given a mild winter.

Ceanothus in many forms can be found for the open ground or to help clothe sunny walls. Some of the hardiest are the deciduous hybrids, such as *Ceanothus* 'Gloire de Versailles', raised in France many years ago. Others, less hardy and evergreen, range from *C. arboreus* 'Trewithen Blue', growing to 12 ft (3.6 m) and more, with bold leaves and blue flowers over a long period, to *C. divergens*, *C. prostratus* and *C. thyrsiflorus*, which are almost ground-clinging

Ceanothus arboreus 'Trewithen Blue' is a vigorous spreading shrub

and suitable for contrasting with the dwarf cotoneasters. 'Trewithen Blue' is often seen as a wall shrub, but it will stand alone in mild districts and, anyway, needs ample wall space. *Ceanothus dentatus*, *C. rigidus*, *C.* 'Autumnal Blue', *C.* 'Southmead' and several others are more compact and suitable for smaller walls.

The south and southerly walls of the house and other buildings are always valuable places on which to grow some of the most tender wall shrubs and climbers. Even there, they may be lost in the rare, usually brief, winter frost, although if there is due warning and action is prompt, temporary protection with netting, hessian, straw or bracken can save many of them. Among others, two cassias, with yellow pea-like flowers, have come through many recent winters with no more than severe cutting back. *Cassia corymbosa* is hardier than *C. obtusa*, but both provide good splashes of yellow in late summer and autumn where they succeed (see p. 58). The New Zealand lobster claw, *Clianthus puniceus*, a straggling shrub with huge pea-like red flowers, needs a warm wall for protection and support. Its white form is less striking unless against a red brick wall. In the angle of a southwest wall, it may be

Clianthus puniceus bears its unusual flowers in spring and early summer

Feijoa sellowiana has the bonus of attractive evergreen leaves with white undersides

worth trying the almost tender *Tibouchina urvilleana* for its large purple flowers that continue through summer (see p. 26). It requires protection in all but the mildest winters. *Itea ilicifolia*, with evergreen holly-like leaves and very long catkins in summer and autumn, will fill quite a large wall and is hardier than some of those mentioned here. Very well drained soil against a warm wall will suit *Feijoa (Acca) sellowiana*, a South American shrub with striking dark red and white flowers and, after the warmest summers, edible egg-shaped fruits.

Some of the relatives of the wind-hardy shrubs already mentioned are not very hardy and do better in the shelter of the mild seaside garden. They include *Olearia × scilloniensis*, which smothers itself every spring with the purest white flowers, and the *O. phlogopappa* 'Splendens' group, producing similar masses of pink, mauve and blue michaelmas daisy-like flowers in the summer. *Olearia semidentata* will be cut to the ground in the colder winters, but often survives for several years and is well worth planting for its larger than usual mauve flowers during early summer. Although some of the hebes, particularly *Hebe dieffenbachii* and *H. × franciscana* 'Blue Gem' and other cultivars, are very wind-hardy, many of the more colourful need the protection of other shrubs or hedges in coastal gardens. Many are hybrids with larger leaves and flower

The flame creeper, *Tropaeolum speciosum*, will climb up to 10 ft (3 m)

spikes: 'Alicia Amherst', 'Miss E. Fittall', 'Purple Queen' and 'Simon Delaux', together with the 'Wand' series in a wide range of colours, all produce valuable flowers over a long period.

Climbers

There are many beautiful climbers and scramblers that add greatly to gardening by the sea, planted among wall shrubs or on suitable bare walls. *Lapageria rosea*, the national flower of Chile, climbs along erect wires or through open shrubs to produce large, delicate, red, pink and white flowers in late summer and autumn. It prefers some shade and ample moisture and, if growing from beneath good ground cover, withstands most winter frosts; in many years the whole plant survives to maintain plentiful aerial growth. Three of the herbaceous tropaeolums will scramble through wall shrubs and others growing in the autumn. *Tropaeolum speciosum*, with scarlet flowers, seems to thrive best in the west of Scotland and is very fickle in approval of its surroundings. Good plants should be planted from pots in late spring and are happiest in the shade of established shrubs in peaty soils. Similarly, *T. tricolorum* and *T. tuberosum* need shade at their roots, the former flowering quite early in the spring and the whole plant dying back before midsummer.

Several of the passion flowers, particularly *Passiflora caerulea*, the hardiest, provide interesting shape and colour on almost any wall. *Berberidopsis corallina*, *Billardiera longiflora*, *Sollya heterophylla* and *Eccremocarpus scaber* can all be allowed to scramble over other wall shrubs, or be trained up bare walls with wire or trellis in the milder districts, and do not overrun either the shrubs or the house. Others should be treated with caution if they are not to smother everything within reach. Most of the actinidias come into this category, particularly *Actinidia deliciosa* (*A. chinensis*), the Chinese gooseberry or kiwi fruit. When male and female plants are grown, fruits can be obtained in warmer areas, but they require at least a two-storey wall or massive poles and strong wire in the open. The least aggressive is the unusual *A. kolomikta*, which has green, pink and white leaves when growing on a wall in full sunshine. Two climbing members of the potato family, *Solanum crispum* and *S. jasminoides* make quite long growth, but can be kept in check without curtailing flowering too much (see p. 63).

Palms and succulents
In addition to the reasonably hardy yuccas (p. 31), other palm-like plants bring variety to the outline of a garden and a sense of the warmer nature of seaside gardens. *Cordyline australis* and *C. indivisa*, often known as dracaena, are among the hardiest, but even they have been killed to ground-level once or twice in living memory in the mildest parts. They have then grown again from below ground and the only problem, after removing the rather stringy dead stumps, is to make sure that the many new shoots are thinned to one, or at most three, in order to preserve their distinctive outlines. They will soon reach sufficient height to allow the large bunches of creamy white, scented flowers to appear early each summer. A similar tree, the Chusan palm, *Trachycarpus fortunei*, has survived where the cordyline has been cut back. It is a true palm, with characteristic leaves clustered at the top of rather thin stems that are covered with the remains of the old leaf stalks. It also carries bunches of flowers each summer. *Chamaerops humilis*, the dwarf fan palm, is the only European native palm, but less hardy than the Chusan. It has similar leaves and flowers and an even

---

Above: *Billardiera longiflora* is a distinctive climber for a partly shaded wall
Below: The dwarf fan palm, *Chamaerops humilis*, does best in a sheltered sunny place

slower-growing stem. Not everyone approves of the shape and often bedraggled appearance of the cordylines and palms, but they certainly make distinctive features in many seaside gardens.

In the mildest gardens, one or two agaves may be planted to provide different shapes with their rosettes of sharp-pointed, tough, succulent leaves. *Agave parryi* is the hardiest and *A. americana* the largest and most exciting. Each grows the rosette for many years and then sends up a single stem, up to 10 ft (3 m) or more tall, with numerous cream-coloured flowers. *Agave americana* is known, rather extravagantly, as the century plant, but although many years elapse before flowering, it is seldom as tardy as implied by the name. After flowering, the original plant dies, usually leaving a cluster of small rosettes which can either remain or be transplanted to fresh sites. More tender and even more striking is the Mexican *Beschorneria yuccoides*, which grows with similar rosettes of pointed leaves. It is perennial and not very frost- or wind-hardy but, in a sheltered spot facing south, it throws rapidly growing, rose pink stems upwards to 8 ft (2.4 m) in early summer every year. The bracts on these striking stems are also pink, while the tiny flowers are bright green.

Scented plants

Many a garden can be improved by the addition of a few plants that contribute scent, either from their foliage in the warmth of the day or when touched in passing, or from their flowers. A tender shrub that does this well is the lemon-scented verbena, *Aloysia triphylla* (*Lippia citriodora*), which will grow into a rather straggling bush when there is not too much frost but is best against a south-facing wall. *Choisya ternata*, a much hardier evergreen, has two very distinct scents – that of the crushed leaves, which is difficult to describe and is not liked by all, and the extremely sweet perfume of the white flowers, which fully justifies the common name of Mexican orange blossom. Several oleasters (pp. 17 and 20) have insignificant white or cream flowers that fill the air with sweet scent in the late summer and autumn. Most of the pittosporums (p. 23) are heavily scented and are particularly noticeable on warm early summer evenings. The commonest, *Pittosporum tenuifolium*, has dark purple, fragrant flowers. The attractive *P. eugenioides* and its variegated form, together with *P. tobira*, are worth their places for their perfume, even if the occasional sharp frost deals harshly with them.

Most of the large number of escallonias so strongly recommended for their wind-hardiness (p. 28) produce a pleasant scent from their foliage on warm summer days. All the myrtles are equally valuable for the fragrance of their flowers. Some, such as *Myrtus communis* and its varieties, are unharmed in all but the coldest winters, but others are less hardy. The least hardy is probably *M. ugni*, with pink flowers and – when sufficient plants are grown – dark red fruits, from which a full flavoured conserve can be made. Between them, the several species available can provide scented flowers for most of the summer. Also fragrant are most of the jasmines. *Jasminum nudiflorum*, the hardy winter species, can be grown almost anywhere but, because of the nature

The succulent *Agave americana* 'Variegata' lends an exotic air to the garden

Buddleia alternifolia makes a graceful shrub or small tree with arching branches

of its growth, looks best on a wall. Some of the others, such as *J. angulare*, *J. mesnyi* and *J. polyanthum*, are good climbers for a warm wall. The common buddleias, *Buddleia alternifolia* and *B. davidii*, are quite hardy and well known for their perfume. *Buddleia asiatica*, equally scented but less hardy, has the advantage of carrying its white flowers well into the autumn in the mildest climates.

Dwarf plants

Certain very low-growing plants, where they can be walked on, also give off scents. The thymes, particularly *Thymus serpyllum* with its many coloured varieties, are quite hardy and are useful in this respect on warmer sites. Less hardy but good in moist spots is the similar close-growing *Mentha requienii*, which will grow in a damp lawn if the grass is kept short. Another very dwarf plant, not scented but interesting in milder gardens, is *Polygonum capitatum*,

Osteospermum jucundum is a perennial in mild areas, with abundant flowers in late summer

which seeds itself to persist after the coldest winters and may come through without harm when frost is less severe. Two genera with daisy-like flowers provide very suitable dwarf plants for seaside gardens – the gazanias, especially the spreading types, and osteospermums, once known as *Dimorphotheca*. Both have given rise to many cultivars from several species, the former with a colour range among the yellows and orange, and the latter from white through pinks to deep purple. They survive mild winters, but are killed by sharp frosts. All strike very easily from cuttings and it is wise to make use of this to carry the plants over the coldest winters.

The ability to propagate vegetatively should really be a feature of any seaside garden where the gardener is tempted to have something of the unusual or, perhaps, to boast a little of the tender plants that he or she is able to grow. Winters in which cherished plants have been killed or cut to the ground leave gaps that have to

47

be filled, either by replacing them with similar plants, or by retreating to the commoner hardy kinds that can be grown anywhere in the country. Although most local nurserymen maintain and propagate stocks of tender plants, many gardeners propagate a few every year as a precaution for their own gardens. Such gardeners tend to put in a few more cuttings than they need and the surpluses are often passed on when the gardens are open or at local plant sales.

THE ORTHODOX GARDEN

So far we have described the two special types of gardening that are available to seaside gardeners – the limited garden of wind-hardy plants and the more exciting but often frustrating garden of half-hardy plants. The two are not exclusive and can be merged into each other. But what of the gardener who does not wish to change?

For those who would garden in the ways that are so common all over the country, there are always limitations wherever they are. Temperatures and humidity vary from the cold of the high hills or high latitudes to the damp of the valleys; rainfall varies from Essex to the Highlands and the Lake District; soils vary, not least in degree of acidity or alkalinity. All have to be taken into account and plants chosen to suit the conditions, unless there is an overriding desire to grow something with a continual battle against the odds. In addition to these general restrictions, there are the effects of the wind and usually the increased moisture that occurs by the sea, which is intensified by the creation of shelter and reduction in wind speeds. Let us look at these problems as they affect the many aspects of gardening in Britain.

Trees and shrubs

Where trees and shrubs are concerned, there is little that can be done to improve their chances. We have discussed those that thrive. Others survive, but some are never really healthy, among them the flowering crabs and cherries and their relatives in the genera *Malus*, *Pyrus* and *Prunus*. Not only are they easily shaped and damaged by wind, but all suffer from fungal and bacterial diseases that are very difficult to keep in check. Few conifers, except those mentioned (p. 14), merit a place unless shelter is ample. Many of them, such as the cypresses, are used to provide the contrast of erect green spires among trees and shrubs, while the spruces and firs are attractive with their Christmas-tree shapes. However, strong winds soon spoil their outline and salt-laden gales brown their foliage.

48

Roses

There are many shrubby roses that will survive and produce satisfactory flowers and hips, some even in quite exposed sites, but the modern hybrids and their relatives are rarely happy unless they receive constant attention. The mild damp atmosphere encourages black spot and mildew is quite prevalent. Fungal diseases can be controlled by regular spraying, but mildewed buds, which are common, are difficult to avoid. Another problem with roses is the length of time that they will remain in growth. They are best lightly pruned in the autumn to reduce the top growth and thus prevent wind-rocking, and then finally pruned rather earlier than usual in the spring. Even so, in many years growth will continue throughout the winter, with the result that the plants need even more generous feeding than usual. Liquid feeding combined with fungal sprays can supplement any farmyard manure and powdered fertilizer that are used.

Roses can be grown by the sea, as at Compton Acres, overlooking Poole Harbour in Dorset, where skilled attention is given

Herbaceous plants

Most herbaceous plants are liable to be blown over unless well sheltered and may tend to be drawn up too high if over-sheltered. Staking the plants is a time-consuming job anyway and is even more difficult in windy situations. Some plants, such as delphiniums, lupins and hollyhocks, are almost impossible. In addition, they are so susceptible to the slugs and snails that proliferate in moist conditions as to make their survival very problematical. The popular hostas also look far from happy with their leaves eaten by these difficult pests. The most likely herbaceous plants to succeed where wind may reach them are those that need no staking, either because they are dwarf and sturdy, or because, like the various forms of astilbe, geum, bergenia, hemerocallis, heuchera and many more, they grow a mat of leaves close the the ground and then send up stiff flower stems for a short while in the summer. The ornamental grasses from among the fescues, holcus and poas may also do well.

Show flowers

The many carnations and pinks, *Dianthus*, rarely thrive unless the soil is alkaline, with a high pH, as on chalk, limestone and calcareous sea sand. Many irises also prefer such conditions to the more acid soils. Of the other common 'show' flowers, good chrysanthemums and dahlias can be grown if there is ample shelter, but with a little more care than may be needed elsewhere, since the moister atmosphere tends to produce more frequent attacks of grey mould (botrytis) on buds and petals. In the mildest districts, dahlias for garden and household decoration can be left in the ground for many years. When they are lifted for winter storage, they should be carefully dried to prevent them rotting in store. Sweet peas are liable to be blown down sometime during the season and the petals damaged unless they are very well sheltered. Daffodils, also a popular show flower, are widely grown around the coasts of Britain. Being quite short and thus easily protected, they are less likely to be damaged by wind and, anyway, can be picked in bud before the flowers can be battered. However, if too well sheltered, the bulbs are more vulnerable to attack by grubs of the large narcissus fly, since the fly enjoys still wind-free conditions in which to fly and lay the eggs which produce the grubs.

Above: dwarf garden hybrids of astilbe, such as 'Atrorosea', grow no more than 18 in. (45 cm) tall
Below: day lilies, *Hemerocallis*, are robust perennials in a wide range of colours

Annuals

In choosing annuals to sow in odd corners or special beds or borders, it will be obvious that shelter must be provided and, in any case, the short low-growing kinds will be preferable to the taller ones. In the sunny conditions that prevail in some coastal districts, many of the dwarf annuals with daisy-like flowers that open more completely in full sunshine are at a great advantage.

Lawns

A lawn is an essential feature of almost every type of garden. There is a modern view that any more or less green mown sward will serve the purpose, or may even be desirable in preserving some native weeds. There is no doubt, however, that a uniform covering of a single grass or similar grasses provides a more satisfactory foil to surrounding plants. Broad-leaved weeds, such as dandelions, daisies and docks, and plants like speedwell, oxalis and wild white clover that flower beneath the level of cutting distract the eye and spoil the appearance of the lawn as a background or foreground. Even variations in grass species, such as Yorkshire fog and annual meadow grass, can be distracting.

In the mild moist conditions of most seaside areas, several aspects of lawn management will need additional attention. Mowing will often have to be continued throughout the year and consequently, with the more frequent removal of the grass, extra fertilizer will be required if a good green sward is to be maintained. Weeds are just as prevalent in seaside lawns and moss tends to grow even more strongly, except on the very sandy soils that sometimes occur. Still windless days on which to apply herbicides are less common. On the other hand, leaf-sweeping is rarely necessary as strong winds regularly bustle the leaves into odd corners, where they can be left or moved to the compost heap.

Tree fruit

Many of the most valuable fruits that can be grown in English gardens are not at their best in seaside gardens. They can be grown – nothing is impossible in gardening – but they often cause more trouble than they are worth or they produce lower-quality crops than can be expected farther inland. New fruit trees, as with all other trees, should be planted as young as possible. Older and larger trees will have great difficulty in producing an adequate root

Sun-loving gazanias are ideal bedding plants for the seaside

system to hold the head of branches, leaves and fruit in windy conditions. Whatever the age, adequate staking is essential in the first years, and the stem or trunk and the stake must be wrapped to prevent chafing.

Apple trees, bushes or trained cordons and espaliers are best pruned by the gardener and not by the wind! Wind-shaped trees will produce fruit of sorts but, unless shelter is provided, the growing of tree fruits is hardly worth contemplating. If flowering coincides with strong winds, the flight of pollinating insects will be reduced and less fruit will result. If autumn gales come before ripening or picking times, as they nearly always do with the later apples and pears, windfalls will be more plentiful and storable crops will be diminished. Even earlier in the summer, the growing fruits may be bruised by being banged against each other and the rasp of leaves can damage the skins of the fruits. Worst of all, the atmosphere near the sea is usually more humid and this encourages

Actinidia deliciosa can be grown for its kiwi fruits in warm parts of Britain, but needs plenty of wall space

scab and canker. The former disease attacks leaves and twigs and spoils the appearance of the fruit, while canker kills twigs, branches and even whole trees. Both diseases can be controlled by spraying, but it must be thorough and generally has to be more frequent in moist conditions than where it is drier, where six or more applications each year are common. Brown rot also seems to be more troublesome in damp conditions, unless the necessary steps are taken to prevent or reduce it. These consist of carefully removing and destroying every affected fruit at the time of picking and removing all fallen fruits from the vicinity of the trees.

Pears present similar problems to apples and really need even more attention almost everywhere in Britain if good-quality fruit is to be grown. They are at their best in warmer climates, as the magnificent fruit we receive from countries farther south demonstrates. Cherries and plums are equally liable to damage by wind and have somewhat similar diseases to those that attack the apple and pear when growing in moist conditions. Heavy rain or a damp atmosphere at ripening time will also encourage fruits to split.

If the seaside gardener is prepared to do without the ornamental shrubs and climbers already recommended for the walls of the house, all these fruit trees will do better there than in the open. Peaches and nectarines, in particular, must have the protection of a wall with a southerly aspect and they also need extra care as regards spraying and shelter from wind. The young shoots due to bear next year's fruit may be broken by the wind if not tied in as they grow. In very mild districts, winter temperatures may not be low enough to break winter dormancy.

Dessert grapes of not very high quality may be grown on south-facing walls in the south and can contribute to a Mediterranean appearance. There are a number of vineyards along the south coast, but they must have shelter and conditions for them are usually better away from the sea breezes which reduce morning and evening temperatures. High temperatures in summer and, particularly, autumn are really essential for production of good wine grapes. The strong climber, *Actinidia deliciosa* (p. 54), will fruit in the milder areas. The New Zealand cultivars 'Bruno' and 'Hayward' are much larger than the species and even more recent ones may be further improvements when they are available. They must have ample length or height of strong wire for the very long vines that they produce.

The common hazel and its cultivated cousins, the cob nut and filbert, need protection from wind, especially at flowering time. If not sheltered, the pollen from the catkins will be blown into the next

parish and will not drop onto the tiny red female flowers that produce the nuts after pollination.

So, it is not an encouraging outlook for orchard fruit by the sea. Those who feel they must grow their own top fruit may either struggle to give all the attention necessary to produce the best possible, or they may provide what shelter they can, plant their orchard and let it grow as it will. In this way, they will provide a good environment for bulbs and other flowers in the grass, and some fruit will arrive in due time. It will not be saleable nor fit for shows, but it may still be better than the 'Golden Delicious' apples or unripe 'Conference' pears from the shops.

Soft fruit

The soft, bush and cane fruits are more feasible given some shelter although, as with tree fruits, the greater dampness of the seaside garden can be a problem. Raspberries and redcurrants are particularly susceptible to wind damage, blackberries, loganberries and hybrid berries, gooseberries and blackcurrants rather less so, but all grow best within good shelter. In all but the most exposed conditions, strawberries are close enough to the ground to avoid serious damage. The uprights and wire on which fruits are trained need to be stronger in windy situations, as does the fruit cage, which is essential if full crops of fruit are to be picked.

Strawberries, raspberries and loganberries are particularly prone to botrytis or grey mould on their fruits in damp seaside conditions and the disease is also likely to increase in the shade cast by the hedges or screens needed for shelter. Spraying can help to reduce damage and the selection of suitable cultivars is useful. Strawberries with smaller leaves and their fruits standing above them, such as 'Pantagruella', and less vigorous raspberries, such as 'Malling Jewel', tend to be less affected than the stronger-growing ones. The autumn-fruiting raspberries are often very successful, but too much rain in September and beyond will cause a complete loss as the grey mould attacks. However, the cultivar 'September' starts to fruit a little earlier than its name implies and than some other autumn croppers, and this usually allows some fruits to be picked before the damp autumn days make the grey mould so tiresome.

Above: the autumn-fruiting raspberry 'September' is worth trying in coastal gardens
Below: bamboos can form an outer screen to protect a vegetable plot

Cassia corymbosa is one of the more tender shrubs for a favoured seaside garden

If loganberries are chosen, the thornless clone is much easier to handle than others and is a heavy cropper. Some of the newer hybrids, particularly 'Tayberry', are far too difficult to deal with, especially in a high wind; this seems to have the prickles of the worst blackberries and the spines of a raspberry. The alternate training system, where blackberry, loganberry and similar canes are tied to one side of the plant as they grow, is better than allowing them to grow over the fruiting canes, as the fruit is left uncovered and therefore drier. Blueberries, from the several American cultivars of *Vaccinium corymbosum*, need really acid soil containing ample peat and the fruit must be protected from birds as well as from strong winds. (For further information, see *The Fruit Garden Displayed*).

Vegetables

The pleasures of eating fresh home-grown vegetables and salads and even of stocking the deep freeze or other stores are not diminished by the seaside. Almost all that is said in *The Vegetable Garden Displayed* applies to gardening by the sea. We will consider the special needs of the seaside garden.

On many coasts, valuable organic matter is there for the taking, and there is no doubt that liberal use of bulky manures is an essential feature of all vegetable gardening. Seaweed carried from the high-tide mark or cut from the rocks has been used for generations to manure near-by farms and gardens. It is heavy, unless allowed to dry, which is difficult on public beaches. It now so often contains unwanted plastics and other undesirable and indestructable debris that it is best sorted as it is collected to avoid cluttering the garden with rubbish. An added disadvantage of seaweed is its attraction for flies that will invade the house and other buildings. For this reason, it is best hauled in winter, when there are fewer flies and the seaweed itself is more plentiful. It can then be spread on uncropped land to be dug in when partially dried, or it can be added to the compost heap, mixed with weeds, hedge trimmings and leaves, and then covered with lawn mowings to encourage decay without encouraging the flies.

On many shores, seaweed is mixed with broken shells that contain much calcium, thus raising the pH of the mixture and making it unsuitable for application to acid-loving plants. It is, however, very welcome in the vegetable garden where the pH is always dropping as calcium is leached from the soil. In some parts of the country, the sea sand comprises a high proportion of finely broken shells and this is regularly used in place of lime or powdered chalk to maintain the best alkalinity for the vegetable crops that need it. Such sand can also improve the physical condition of heavier soils.

Wind has already been mentioned – some may say too often – but it is an ever-present problem, not least in several vegetable garden practices. Unless the vegetable garden is fully sheltered, runner beans will be difficult to keep erect on the usual tall sticks and the field method, of allowing suitable cultivars to run along the ground with their tips removed regularly, may be a better system. It does not produce such long straight pods, but the crop can be just as heavy. Similarly, dwarf peas growing on the ground may be better than tall ones on sticks or string. If sticks are to be used, they must be strong and have a few extra cross bracings to hold the rows together, or pea boughs may be supported on wires strained to strong poles at the ends of the rows.

It is often desirable to earth up the taller winter brassicas, such as brussels sprouts and sprouting and winter broccoli. Planted in shallow drills drawn with a hoe, they are first supported as the earth is levelled in hoeing and then supported by earthing up, almost as for potatoes. The mildest districts allow regular cropping of winter cauliflower or broccoli from November to May, and most other winter brassicas can be relied on to survive and continue in growth throughout the winter, when the shallow ridge and furrow thus created not only supports the stems but provides a certain amount of drainage.

It is rare that frost is so hard beside the sea that the usual early-sown vegetables will not overwinter. However, broad beans, sown in the late autumn, can be so battered by wind and swirled around in muddy little holes that they die of drowning instead of frost. Later sowing in boxes or pots under glass, for planting in early spring, may often be better, but even then protection is required. Winter lettuce, winter spinach and spring onions can all be blown to pieces where strong winds sweep across exposed gardens. While ripe onions need to be lifted and thoroughly dried for hanging in a dry shed for the winter, other root vegetables such as beet and parsnips can be left, as they are unlikely to be frozen into the ground.

Although the milder conditions allow many crops to survive the winter and others to be sown and planted earlier, all but the lightest soils are difficult to prepare in the heavier rainfall and fewer drying days that prevail. There is also very little frost to break up the surface after autumn digging. Early digging or merely clearing and levelling and no digging, to leave the minimum of large clods on heavy soils, may be the answer. If, when the time comes for early sowing or planting, the surface is too wet and difficult to work, the use of boards on which to walk beside the proposed line of sowing will avoid damaging the tilth; the spread of the weight on the boards does much less damage than the feet direct on the soil. Another way to prepare for sowing is to place a line of cloches over the intended row a week or two before sowing. This will dry the surface slightly and many crops will benefit from further cover if the cloches are replaced after sowing. Early potatoes, broad beans, peas, summer cabbage and cauliflower, carrots, turnips, green onions and beet-root can all be obtained much earlier from January to February sowings in this way. Some of them may be harvested even earlier from greenhouse sowing in pots or boxes, followed by early planting.

Cloches, frames and plastic tunnels are useful aids to early production of vegetables and salads in any garden. In exposed situations, they are at risk and special precautions are necessary, using strong cords to hold down frames and plastics, or providing local shelter to protect them. The older glass cloches usually remain firm once they have settled in, except in the teeth of the worst gales. It is a good plan, however, to draw a light drill on each side of the line of cloches when they are moved, so they can settle in more quickly and remain firm. Tunnels or cloches of pliable plastic are not usually damaged unless there is an opening or tear where the wind can enter and blow away the whole row. In the same way, an open door or ventilator on the windward side of a greenhouse will allow pressure to build up and blow out glass on the other side. Even the overlapping glass admits some air and produces similar pressure and it has been found worthwhile to open ventilators on the lee side to reduce the pressure and the risk of damage.

The damp atmosphere in seaside gardens encourages potato blight disease earlier in the season and more regularly than in drier districts. (It also affects tomatoes.) Spraying to prevent attacks, whenever moist mild conditions arrive, is essential if potatoes have not reached lifting time, and for tomatoes – even under glass – if potatoes are growing nearby. Spraying will also be necessary for mid-season and maincrop potatoes, if they are grown, although it is doubtful if they are worth it in small gardens. Earlies can, as we have mentioned, be planted earlier and have their haulms cut off before blight begins to appear because, unless spraying is thorough and frequent, it is of little use in the mild wet days of a seaside summer.

CONCLUSION

Almost any plant can be grown in nearly any situation with the necessary time, skills and money to provide the right conditions. To go to extremes, such as the commonly stated example of bananas at the North Pole, is to invite continuous struggle, frustration and expenditure. The number of specialist societies and books about individual plants indicates that there are many who must concentrate on their own speciality, and it is hoped that these notes will help them to overcome the problems if they insist on bringing their hobby to the seaside. Others may wish to create all the features of a

former garden. For them, the reduction of wind-damage and related difficulties may be of assistance, but it is suggested that the two main variations – the wind-hardy garden and the half-hardy garden – may have greater attractions.

The seaside garden, of whatever size, can be as varied as any other with the planned aid of ample protection from wind, salt and driven sand. In addition, it is possible to experiment with the many varied and truly exotic plants that can only be admired in foreign parts or heated greenhouses and are impossible to grow in colder gardens.

Opposite: *Solanum jasminoides*, a beautiful summer-flowering climber for the half-hardy garden

Below: Glendurgan, a sheltered garden on the Helford estuary in Cornwall

Cpu

Gardens to Visit

The following is a selection of gardens situated on or near the coast. Many seaside resorts also have interesting gardens on the edge of the sea, and useful ideas can be gleaned from both. (NT = National Trust; NGS = National Gardens Scheme; NTS = National Trust for Scotland).

England
Abbotsbury Gardens, Abbotsbury, Dorset (NGS)
Compton Acres, Poole, Dorset (NGS)
Glendurgan, Mawnan Smith, Cornwall (NT)
Headland, Battery Lane, Polruan, Cornwall (NGS)
Liverpool University Botanic Gardens, Ness, Neston, S Wirral
Overbecks Museum & Garden, Sharpitor, Salcombe, Devon (NT)
St Michael's Mount, Marazion, Cornwall (NT, NGS)
Trebah, Mawnan Smith, Cornwall (NGS)
Trengwainton, Penzance, Cornwall (NT)

Channel Islands
La Colline, Jersey

Isles of Scilly
Tresco Abbey, Tresco

Wales
Plas Newydd, Isle of Anglesey, Gwynedd (NT)

Scotland
Achamore Gardens, Isle of Ghiga, Strathclyde
Brodick Castle, Isle of Arran, Strathclyde (NTS)
Dunrobin Castle, Golspie, Highlands
Inverewe, Poolewe, Highlands (NTS)
Kiloran, Isle of Colonsay, Strathclyde
Logan Botanic Garden, Port Logan, Dumfries & Galloway (Royal Botanic Garden, Edinburgh)